The Alive Sales Rep

Live Your Life. Eliminate Stress. Close More Sales

by Brandon Hensinger

ISBN: 978-0-578-06058-3

First Edition, February 2011

Library of Congress Cataloging-In-Publication:

Brandon Hensinger. The Alive Sales Rep. Ascent Publishing. 2011.

Sales Training, Business, Self Help

100 pages

Printed in the United States

ISBN 978-0-578-06058-3

90000

9 780578 060583

Dedicated to

My wife Megan, my kids Lydia and Seth, and to all of the Sales Reps that I have the privilege of working with throughout the years.

Table of Contents

Chapter 1: Why I Wrote This Book

Why did I write this book? What is this book about?

Simple. I have learned how to have exceptional sales success by breaking away from the old model and view of sales and adapting a new one in which I can live a great life, eliminate stress, and close more sales (which translates into making more money!). I have had a growing desire to share the things I have learned, so other sales reps also can feel and experience the difference.

I have become tired of reading book after book on how to close more sales. I have grown tired of sales training companies only teaching how to present, close, prospect, etc. It is time for a book that teaches sales reps how to manage life and work in a way that eliminates stress, and helps them to live life, because that is a guaranteed way to close more sales!

The Alive Sales Rep is a combination of practical tools and theory that will help those who read it to dramatically improve their life and sales success.

Here is my story:

I have been a sales rep for almost 10 years now in various industries ranging from rental car sales, to pharmaceutical sales, and medical sales rep jobs. Over the past several years I began to realize increasingly how I and other reps around me were consumed with our work…especially during non-work hours. As a sales rep it was so easy, and seemed so necessary to take my work home with me mentally and physically since it seemed like clients always had needs and because the harder and more continuously I worked, I assumed the more commission I'd make and the more recognition I'd get.

I quickly became consumed with constantly checking emails, working on forecasts, planning and analyzing my territory, working through my sales tracking system, and thinking about work constantly. I tried to always keep track of the hundreds of projects and tasks that I had on my plate, while continuing to hit the streets making sales calls. I felt like hiring my own sales outsourcing company so that I could get some assistance!

The amazing thing is that I successfully did all of that, so never thought twice about the fact that I was stressed out constantly, had no work life balance, and wasn't enjoying all the things in life that I once did.

Over time I started to realize that because I was living for work, my life was suffering. I then asked the question:

"Since I am unbalanced in my work life, and it has a negative affect on my life, is my work unknowingly suffering as well? If I found balance, would I be more successful at work AND life?"

At first it seemed like I would be spinning an endless number of plates, but surely there was a way to do it. I became tired of reading book after book teaching me how to close a sale. I became tired of the way reps had been doing the same thing for decades.

This old model and view of sales would be hard to change.

So I made it my mission to accomplish the following elementary things:

- •Learn how to be disciplined to leave work at work and enjoy life at home.

- •Find ways to automate my sales call scheduling and territory planning.

- •Find ways to manage the millions of thoughts and tasks I had running through my head always.

- •Find time to enjoy all the things I once did.

I began to develop systems that helped me accomplish these things. Some I learned from others, some I created on my own.

What happened? My sales SKYROCKETED! I quickly outperformed those around me. I doubled my income in only 1 year! I had VPs of my company comment that they were amazed to see how much I had grown and how my success so quickly increased. They wanted to know how I did it!

What about in my personal life? My rock climbing ability greatly increased (that is my sport of choice), I learned jazz guitar, travelled to Asia, Africa, Europe, and other national locations, had 2 kids, bought a house, and have a weekly date night with my wife!

So I accomplished what I wanted:

- A love for my work

- A great work life balance

- Remarkable life experiences

- Huge sales success

After years of working on this, my notes and plans have turned in to what I believe to be the most important book a sales rep will ever read. It is a combination of a life coaching course and sales training course, and will give you a great tool to begin the journey towards a more enjoyable life, less stress, and greater sales success!

Chapter 2: Work to Live, Don't Live to Work

The purpose of this book is to set sales reps on the path towards greater enjoyment of life, no stress, and greater sales. One of the foundational principles that needs to be addressed and applied is learning to not make your life about work. The rest of this book gives guidelines and tools for sales reps to use and follow to help them accomplish this switch in paradigm. The profession of sales lends itself to this mentality so easily because our livelihoods depend upon commission. We need to take care of current business, sell new business, and do a ton of administrative work. So of course this additional pressure makes us feel that we need to do work all the time. There is a common sentiment among sales reps (and other business people as well), that if you don't have a "live to work" mentality (i.e. working all the time), that you are being lazy and won't be as successful. The idea of not working all time sounds foreign to most sales reps. That's why I feel that it is so important that sales reps begin to understand how dangerous it is to live this way. That's why I want to write this book. I want to help sales reps escape from this dangerous paradigm, and begin to experience the success and happiness that comes from adopting a new "Work to Live" paradigm.

Let's start by addressing some important questions.

So Why Do You Work in the First Place?

This is a question that I bet you have never asked yourself. If you have, then you are already on the right track to becoming alive! Before you read on, get a piece of paper, or your phone/email device, and get ready to write down the answer to these 2 questions.

"What is my time and life consumed by?"

"Why Do I Work?"

The first question was probably easy to answer. The second question...probably not. If you find yourself struggling to answer that question, you aren't alone and you shouldn't feel worried that you can't answer it. You are in the same boat as most people. If we aren't motivated by the right things, it's hard to find an answer to that question that is satisfactory. In asking this question, we are not looking for a surface answer, but rather looking for root motivation. What drives you to work in the way you do?

Maybe this answer resonates within you: "I work because my life is all about work." In other words, the reason you work so much is because you have systematically made your life about work. You can't imagine anything else in your life being more important to you than work. You don't find fulfillment in getting work done; you find fulfillment in the work itself. You fill every moment you have with work until you are so used to it, that it feels abnormal to not work. So your life becomes about work. You live to work. Taking time to meditate on this question of "Why do I work" could possibly be depressing as you realize that you are working non stop simply because your life is defined by work.

Often, the reason so many people create lives for themselves that are consumed by work is because there is so much work to do. The common sentiment among many is "If I could work 24 hours per day, I would definitely have enough work to fill that time and still not be done." Would you say the same about food? What if someone asked an overweight person "Why do you eat so much?" They could say, "Because there is so much food to eat," when in reality that is not the reason. The reason they eat so much is because they feel like they need to eat as much as possible to feel fulfilled. In reality, they could eat the perfect amount and still be fulfilled. Just because the food is there doesn't mean it has to constantly be consumed.

So here we are at the point of realizing that it is hard to find an answer to the question of "Why do I work?" If it is hard for you to find an answer, chances are that you are living to work instead of working to live. What if you changed that around? What if you begin to work to live instead? Your answer would change instantly. You could say: "I work so that I can enjoy my life, and provide the resources and means to do and accomplish the things I am personally interested in and passionate about." That would make such a difference. You wouldn't be working for work's sake. Rather, you would be working for LIFE's sake. Instead of feeling like you need to sacrifice personal time and interests to get work done outside of normal work hours, you would begin to think, "I need to make sure I am not working late at night so that I can spend time with my family, or exercise, or [insert your personal like here]. This is the backbone to becoming an alive sales rep. So...how much of your personal life and enjoyment have you given up for the sake of work? Have you ever told yourself, "No, I'm not going to work after hours because I have personal interests in...?"

The Backbone of the Alive Sales Rep

The idea of Working to Live and Not Living to Work is the backbone of this book and to the life of a successful sales rep. By correcting the path that you are on, and beginning to see life and work through this paradigm, you will eliminate stress, enjoy life, AND close more sales. That is the goal of this book. I will provide you with tools and mental processes to move into a work to live lifestyle.

Eliminate Stress

Being an alive sales rep starts here. Eliminating stress is of utmost importance. One of the greatest reasons for the overwhelming stress in a sales reps life is the fact that sales reps make their lives about work. Life is not meant to be about work, so when it is forced to become that way, stress ensues. Changing to a work to live paradigm will naturally eliminate stress. There are practical steps that sales reps can take, as well as beliefs to change to eliminate stress.

Enjoy Life

This goes without saying. When you work to live, you will enjoy life 100 times more. This is because your life will start to be about living instead of working. You will start to see your work as part of your life, not the all defining aspect of your life.

Close More Sales

By changing your paradigm to a "Work to Live" paradigm, you will begin to be motivated by goals that matter to you. Having a fulfilling life and accomplishing the things you desire is a much more powerful motivation that wanting to climb the corporate ladder or just working for work's sake. If you begin to work to live, your sales will sky rocket because you will be motivated to work hard and close more sales so that you can accomplish what you want to personally and in your life. You will also have MUCH more energy to work hard if you only work during certain hours instead of around the clock.

The idea is profound, but simple.

The following chapters will walk you through what you need to start doing to become an alive sales rep. Here's how we will do it:

- **Start with internal change by exposing 10 myths that sales reps believe and learn how to conquer them**. You must realize that changing external behaviors, without changing internal behaviors is fruitless. It's like trying to make an apple tree grow good fruit by taping apples to the branches, when in reality the roots are rotten in the first place. It will never produce good fruit.
- **Begin to develop new external sales behaviors and lifestyles behaviors** that grow out of the internal change that takes place. Only when you change the way you think, can you begin to make external changes that last.

So, let's get started by briefly discussing the importance of internal change before external change.

Chapter 3: Out of the Heart the Mouth Speaks

I want to go one step further in discussing why I am addressing these internal changes first.

Sales reps are known for talking. Rightfully so, considering most of our work is done by talking! Therefore, the truth that "Out of the heart the mouth speaks," is more applicable to sales reps than any other person in any other profession. To be an effective sales rep, we must first change what is going on inside. I want to take that a step further and say that out of the heart the mouth speaks and the body acts. All of our actions and words are determined by what is going on inside of us first.

So, let's say that you want to become an apple farmer. You don't have much money, so you get some trees from another apple farmer that donated them to you. So you plant them. Then, you want to instantly get fruit, so you tape apples to the tree. When people come to see your orchard, they are amazed at how beautiful the trees look. However, eventually, those apples will die, as well as the trees, because you didn't address what was most important: cultivating the roots. Taping apples to the tree will do nothing. Good fruit, of course, that you and others can enjoy, will be on the tree for a while, but it will fall off soon since it isn't real. If you cultivate the roots, however, then real, beautiful apples will grow.

The same is true with us. We can put all kinds of processes, actions, practices, etc., in place in our lives and look like we are super productive, super happy, and super successful, while in reality inside we are so scattered and so stressed out, that eventually all the external things will collapse because we haven't focused on what really matters...cultivating ourselves and our internal practices first.

So maybe you think that your fruit in your life is great: You've been successful at sales, people are always praising you, you have all the material things you want., but have you ever stopped and considered how you're doing internally? So many wrong beliefs about sales have most likely been engrained in to you, causing you to have bad roots, and therefore not produce the quality of fruit that you are capable of. It's like CS Lewis said, we can be "like an ignorant child who is content making mud pies in the slum because he cannot imagine what is meant by a holiday at the sea."[1] You may be content where you are and not realize how much better you can be because you simply don't know what else is out there.

That's why in this book, I am deviating from the normal approach to sales books, which is to give "how to close" advice. I want to start deeper. We need to start at the heart, where the words and actions come from in the first place. If we don't first begin to change ourselves internally, we will never be able to change our paradigm to a work-to-live paradigm.

---

[1] C.S. Lewis, Mere Christianity (HarperCollins, 1952) n. pag

Chapter 4: 10 Sales Myths to Stop Believing

It's Time for a New Paradigm of Sales

Alright...what you are about to read is a direct challenge to some of the most popular sayings, beliefs, practices and conventional sales wisdom that exists today. I have spent years observing and practicing these popular, outdated items, and have come to realize that no one seems to ever challenge them or to think through whether they are really helpful beliefs and practices. It seems to me that phrases like "It's a numbers game," get passed down from generation to generation and are just accepted without question. I am going to challenge you to read through these items and reevaluate your sales paradigm.

If corrected in your life, these will be the most important belief changes you can make to set your self on the path to live life, eliminate your stress, and close more sales. Believing these myths are what cause a sales rep's life to be consumed by work. Change your beliefs about these areas and you will see that your time will be better used, and you will feel burdens lifted off of your shoulders, and you will also see your sales skyrocket.

Of course, these things might rock your world and you will feel overwhelmed by the implications. Just start out small. Take one at a time and chew on it. I promise that if you begin to think for yourself and form your own beliefs and practices, your sales will improve phenomenally. So here goes. Time to debunk some myths.

Make sure you take time to also see the worksheets in the appendix as they will give you specific exercises to perform to help you apply the myth-correction guidelines below.

Myth #1: Sales is a Numbers Game

Truth #1: Sales is an Ideal Customer Game (Actually...it's Not a Game at All)

I can pretty much guarantee that every sales rep out there has heard and has engrained this phrase into their minds. Also, I am sure that there are people reading this now thinking that I am crazy for even challenging this idea, but since you have made it this far reading, it means you are interested in changing your sales beliefs, so please keep reading. First, let me define what this phrase has traditionally meant: the more sales calls that a rep makes, the more closes will take place. It's a numbers game. So the rep must find every prospect that remotely fits the target market and call on every one of them. I do agree that you need to make sales calls to close more sales. Of course. That's a no brainer. What I *disagree* with is the belief that sheer volume of calls will lead to more sales.

This is the number one myth that if believed will cause you to be overworked. In fact, if this belief isn't changed, it will prevent you from being able to truly apply anything else from this book. The idea here is that by changing your beliefs and practices regarding this phrase, you will feel much less pressed for time and therefore make much more effective sales calls because you will be focused on the sales calls themselves instead of how you need to squeeze more in to the day. In fact, *you will close more sales by focusing on the truth of sales being an ideal customer game.*

I believe that successful sales will only come when the sales rep stops believing the "Numbers Game Myth" and starts approaching their sales call strategy differently. Introducing the 80/20 rule. It says that 80% of your business comes from 20% of your prospects. If you stop calling on every single prospect, and focus your efforts on those prospects that will give you the greatest return, then you can be certain that calling on a high volume of these prospects will lead to bigger closes and more sales. Look at it this way: As a sales rep, you know that the amount of time taken up making sales pitches to, closing, and setting a small client is no different from the amount of time taken up with a larger client. You know what types of clients take up too much time and resources. I bet as you read this you can think of exactly the type of your prospects and our clients that I refer to. Therefore, wouldn't it be smarter to focus your energy on those clients that will have the highest return on your time investment?

I reiterate what I said above: *The idea here is that by changing your beliefs and practices regarding this phrase, you will feel much less pressed for time and therefore make much more effective sales calls because you will be focused on the sales calls themselves instead of how you need to squeeze more in the rest of the day. You will close more sales and will close higher dollar sales.*

Challenge:

- Get your list of prospects.

- Get out a piece of paper (or better yet, create an Evernote [www.evernote.com] note, or Word document) and list the criteria that make for an ideal client. To do this, try to write a paragraph describing the ideal client. "My ideal client is one who....and does...etc."

- Now go through your list of prospects. How many of those prospects fit your criteria? How many don't?

These are the prospects that you should be calling on. By completing this exercise, you will reduce the number-of-sales-calls burden, and know that you are making smart sales calls.

It isn't a numbers game. It's an Ideal Customer Game. By calling on ideal customers, you will close more sales. By choosing the criteria for your ideal customer, and filtering your prospects based on these ideal criteria, you will make smarter sales calls, not more sales calls, and your return on time investment will drastically increase. You will escape from the stress of worrying that you missed one small prospect, because you know that you have found and are calling on all the big ones.

The intention here is not only to close more sales. Remember: your goal is to eliminate stress, close more sales, and live life. Changing your beliefs and practices in this area will significantly decrease stress because you will not be burdened by meaningless tasks, you will be certain that you are strategically selling to your prospects, and your time occupied by work (that is, the time occupied outside of the normal work hours) will, I guarantee, significantly decrease.

Myth #2: Multi Tasking Should Always Be Used

Truth #2: Uni Tasking Will Get More Done...Guaranteed

Sales reps are infamous for multi tasking. Blackberries always on hand, we check emails constantly, while making phone calls, listening to voicemails, taking sales notes, reading articles, etc.

Multi tasking is the only way to get all of our work done, right? Wrong.

By switching back and forth between tasks, we often forget important details, and our work loses quality. The mind can in fact only focus on one thing at a time. We are not the computers we think we are. Right now, I am sitting here writing this and my iPhone is next to me buzzing away. I just had 2 phone calls, 5 emails, and 1 text message come through in the past 30 minutes. I only have about 30 minutes of time left today to write. If I took time to listen to voicemails right now and read the emails and texts while writing, I would write significantly less, and have much less focus than if I just stay on task.

Challenge

Here is an exercise for you to complete to see why multitasking doesn't work. Dave Crenshaw has a book called <u>The Myth of Multitasking</u>. I borrow this exercise from him:

- Take out a piece of paper and write "Multitasking is a lie" at the top

- Now, draw 4 lines below it

- Get a stopwatch

- You are going to time yourself doing the following: Write "Multitasking is a lie" on the first line. Do it by writing one letter at a time, and following each letter, write a number on the second line. So you would write M, then 1 underneath it, U, then 2 underneath it, L, then 3 underneath it, etc., until you complete the phrase. How long did it take you? Did you make errors? Add 1 second for each error.

- Now time yourself again, this time writing the full sentence on line 3, and then writing the numbers on line 4 (not alternating between letters and numbers this time). How long did it take you? Did you make errors? Chances are you did it MUCH faster, and had no errors.

By completing this simple exercise, you should see that doing one task to completion at a time will allow you to complete much more, without errors, in less time. [2]

Multitasking will not make you more successful. It is a hindrance. Work on one thing at a time until completion. You will get more done as a result and, most importantly, the things you do get done will be done to 100% completion and to the best of your ability. Now, not multi tasking does require, in my opinion, an external task management system so that you can keep record of things to be done without having to think about them constantly. I will write more on that later, so suffice it to say that you need to start disciplining yourself to STOP multi tasking and take action to do one task at a time.

---

[2] Dave Crenshaw, The Myth of Multitasking (Jossey-Bass, 2008) n. pag.

Myth #3: I Must Talk About Every Detail with Every Prospective Client Since it May Be the Only Chance I Have to Talk to Them.

Truth #3: More Options Will Lead to More Confusion.

Sales reps often think that if they don't get to say every benefit and value of their product that they will lose the sale and that the prospect will miss key decision making points. So in a matter of 10 minutes, 15 benefits are delivered, and the rep expects that the prospect will be impressed and that they will close the sale. This couldn't be farther from the truth. I have seen so many sales reps sit and talk to a prospect, oblivious to the fact that they have lost the prospects attention after the first point.

Think about your experience in your personal life when you shop either online or at the mall. What kind of company are you most likely to buy an item or service from? Most likely your answer is that you buy from the company that makes your decision easy and simple. That's why Apple has become so popular as compared to Microsoft. There are so many varieties of Microsoft Windows based computers, and software etc. Apple says "Here is what we offer, and it's better because it's simpler and you have fewer decisions to make." If you have a Mac, you probably understand what I mean!

The same is true with our jobs and sales pitches. Learn what your customer needs and then target them with what matters!

Remember, sales is about the client, not about you and how much you can say or squeeze in to a presentation. To close the sale, the client has to remember what you say, and find you likable, not an annoying information dumper! Think about the last time you got a telemarketer phone call. Were you willing to listen to them rattle on and on?

Imagine how much simpler following up would be. You could say "Last time we talked about [1 or 2 things]," as opposed to "Last time we talked about [xxxxxxxxxxxxxx] (if you even remember all you talked about...because they sure won't."

Keep your sales presentations simple and talk to the client only about what you are certain they are interested in. Make your sales pitches more of a conversation. This will allow you be more relaxed before, during, and after a presentation. By taking this approach, you will avoid the "OH NO! I forgot to tell them xxxxx!" thought after the sales call.

We often think, as sales reps, that by providing many choices, the client will more likely find something that they like. Many companies provide so many options, and so many possible combinations, that it often makes it impossible to remember and/or choose the right products or services. Also, when we provide ourselves with too many options for sales organization, etc., we also end up confusing ourselves.

This goes two ways.

- When we have too many options to sell, we often become confused ourselves and forget what exactly it is we are selling. This causes stress and causes us to lose focus.

- When we have too many options to sell, clients often are unsure about buying because they don't know if they made the right decisions.

Tim Ferriss brings up the following points:

- Too many choices = less or no productivity

- Too many choices = less or no appreciation

- Too many choices = sense of overwhelm[3]

When we offer too many choices to a client, we are making ourselves less effective as sales reps, and causing our clients to struggle with their decision making. Remember, we want to make things easier for our clients, and we want to make ourselves more efficient sales reps. You can be sure that your competitors are in your clients' offices trying to bring doubt into their mind regarding your product. Realize that if you are offering your client too many options, then you are catering to that doubt. You are the sales rep. You are the consultant. Start being the one to teach your clients what their best choice is. Give them guidance. Help them make decisions. They will value you and your guidance so much more and most importantly will be confident in the decision they have

---

[3] Timothy Ferris, <u>Four Hour Workweek</u> (Crown Publishing, 2009) n. pag.

made. Limit the options and choices you present to your prospects. You will be more focused and they will be more satisfied.

Now, this also applies, as mentioned above, to the options we give ourselves as sales reps. If we are following Myth #1, and seeing sales as a numbers game, we are giving ourselves too many options for prospects. We will be confused and less focused. If we are following Myth #2, we are giving ourselves too many things to work on at once. We will be overwhelmed and confused, and our quality of work will suffer.

Okay, so how does changing this belief allow the sales rep to live life (i.e. free up time), eliminate stress, and close more sales? By paying more attention to what really matters to the prospect, you will spend less time preparing large presentations, less time presenting to the client, and will have a much more relaxed approach to sales. Also, the discipline of preparing for a sales call with only the material you need will help you learn to me more confident and to stop doubting yourself. That will most definitely carry over in to all of life.

Challenge

- Ask more questions. Learn more about the prospects situation. Find out what kind of problems and issues they are having with their current product and/or service. This will help you narrow down your list of benefits.

- Recall the fact that most people will forget what you say if you give them more than 3 things to remember.

- When making your sales call, leave all the things you aren't presenting in your office/car/home so that you aren't tempted to information dump. You might be thinking, "But what if they ask me about [product] and I don't have the information? I HAVE to bring all my info with me." You need to start thinking differently. You need to be the one in control of the sales presentation, so be confident that the information you have with you and that you have prepared will be sufficient. In the case that they ask for info that you don't have, still answer their questions, and look at it as a guaranteed opportunity to follow up. You can ask them, "Do you mind if I follow up with you laster today/tomorrow with that info?"

Myth #4: Thinking that Cold Calling is Alive

Truth #4: Cold Calling is Dead

Cold calling is dead. In today's world, with the arrival of things like Spam blockers, Do Not Call Lists, DVRs, Blogs, Online Magazines, Google Ads, etc., consumers are able to block out unwanted ads. People do not want to be bothered with sales messages being pushed upon them. What people do want is valuable information that is of a benefit to them, often that they seek out. Look at all the social media and social networking. People use Twitter, RSS Feeds, etc., to get the information they want that they are certain will improve their lives and business. Sales reps need to stop approaching prospects by cold calling.

I propose a new methodology. It's called **Value Calling.** Sales reps needs to bring value to their prospects. This means not just sitting down and rattling through all the new product/company can do for the prospect, but rather providing something for the client that will make them see the rep as a valuable source of information and will welcome and appreciate their opinions. This will create trust and will ultimately lead to the client buying from the sales rep long term.

Does this sound like a daunting task to you? Maybe that's because you don't know your clients or prospects well enough! Starting there is best...get to know your prospects and clients so that you can talk with them about what matters to them, not to you.

Challenge:

- Medical/Pharmaceutical Reps: Bring interesting articles for the doctors. Talk to them about these articles and/or research and not only your product. Make them look forward to seeing you.

- Insurance Reps: Give your prospects information on living healthy lives, or improving quality of life. Make them see that you are valuable to all of their life and happiness.

- Retail Sales: Instead of saying, "How can I help you?", approach customers saying, "Hey this would look GREAT on you."

Hopefully you get the picture. Make prospects WANT to see you.

Value Calling is what prospects want. You need to make your prospects want and appreciate your visits. By selling in this way, it will help you enjoy visiting your clients and prospects, and it will cause you to eliminate the stress of "What am I supposed to talk about?" because you will always have something ready for them to promote VALUE.

Myth #5: You Need to Work 20 Hours a Day

Truth #5: Work is Most Effective if Done During Work Hours

Parkinson's Law says *"Work expands so as to fill the time available for its completion."* In other words, if you limit the time that you work, you will get much more done. Work finds a way to fit in to the time you give it. Therefore if you work 12 hours a day, you will find 12 hours worth of work to do.

Sales reps are notorious for overworking. I know I sure spent countless hours at night and very early morning working, all because I needed to get everything done and thought there was no other way to do it. However, I began to realize that the reason I was so overwhelmed with work was because I dedicated so many hours to it.

By working 12+ hour days, I in a sense dug my own hole because I made myself used to having that much work to do. Work made itself stretch out into 12 hours and I kept trying to add more and it kept increasing my hours.

I soon decided as I decided what my work hours would be (typically 10 hours) to say "Here are the hours I will work," and became discipline with time spent working. Soon, I found that I was getting 100% of the work done that I needed to. The work fit the time that it had available. Does that mean that at the end of the day, there was nothing left undone? No. It just meant that it would be okay to come back to it the next day in work time. It is okay to get to a finishing *point* and come back to complete the project the next day. It is not procrastination. It is prioritization. If you prioritize appropriately, you will never need to procrastinate.

Challenge

- Over the next 2 weeks, keep accurate records of how much time you work. This includes how much time you think about work related tasks as well. At the same time, keep track of how many things you leave undone or procrastinate each day.

- At the end of 2 weeks, note how many hours per day you worked on average, and how many things you left undone each day on average

- Now for the next 2 weeks, limit your work hours intentionally (7-6, 8-6, 9-5....whatever works best for you).

- Keep track of the hours you work accidentally outside of those hours (i.e. sending emails, thinking about work). Also take note of undone items.

I guarantee that by the end of this experiment, you will notice that you accomplished at least 50% more, and felt 1000x less stressed out and overwhelmed limiting your work hours to a reasonable amount.

You know what I also bet on? That at the end of this experiment, the amount of leisure activities you participated in increased, and you will begin to get your personal life back on track!

Myth #6: Paper Based Organization Methods are Useful

Truth #6: Paper Based Organization Methods Will Make You Less Effective and Cause You More Stress

Do you carry around a massive crate in your trunk with paper files and folders on every client? Are you ever somewhere where you wish you had certain files, but don't. Then you forget to look up that information when you get back to where your files are? Have you ever lost important papers? What do you do with emails sent to prospects? Do you forget pens sometimes and not have a place to make notes? Do you ever run out of notebook paper?

This is a matter of opinion. With the technology that is available today, I believe that NO sales rep should be relegated to paper systems. Sales reps need to find electronic systems that allow them to do the following:

• Have important files always available

• Have client notes and information with them

• Have important prospect contact names information with them

- Access voicemail and emails

- Task management

- Never forget important information or items

By making yourself electronically mobile in these areas, you literally increase your productivity by 100%. Here are some recommendations I make.

I MUST MAKE A POINT OF CLARIFICATION: I am sort of breaking my previously mentioned myth by offering too many options below. I am not breaking the rule. Due to the volume of people reading this info, I do not know what will work best for every person. For example, I use Apple's iDisk, but many people don't have Macs. I use QuickOffice for iPhone. Many people don't have iPhones. So I am simply offering lists of other similar services. What I INSIST on is that you do not eliminate any of the categories. You must have an electronic file system, CRM, note taking, and task management system.

My process consists of the following. I manage all clients and prospects and deals in SalesForce CRM. I take notes from meetings and brainstorming notes in Evernote Mobile App, which syncs with my computer and web based account. I use Apple's iDisk to sync all my files. I use RememberTheMilk.com for task management.

Files

- iDisk - Mac users can subscribe to iDisk to synchronize their hard drives with a remote hard drive (iDisk). This way, no matter where they are, any computer can access that website and download files, email files, and share files. In fact, the iPhone can access iDisk directly to view and share files.

- Pages, Numbers, and Keynote - Apple has now launched their Pages, Numbers, and Keynote apps for the iPhone and iPad. This app integrates with iDisk, and is the most robust office document editing app available. It allows you to edit Word, Excel, Powerpoint, and if you use Apple's productivity suite, Pages, Numbers, and Keynote files. You can upload changes to iDisk, and email files directly from the app. They can be exported as the original file type, or as a PDF. To me, the ability to export as a PDF is the greatest feature.

- DropBox - If you don't have iDisk, or don't have a Mac, you can use DropBox to synchronize all important files between your computer and a remote disk. This way, no matter where they are, any computer can access that website and download files, email files, and share files. Blackberries and iPhones can access DropBox directly to view and share files.

- GoogleDocs - Similar the iDisk and DropBox. This also allows for group collaboration on single documents. So instead of emailing documents back and forth for a team to work with, the entire team can access one document and make changes in real time.

- QuickOffice and DocumentsToGo - These are mobile office suites that will allow you to edit and email Word, Excel, and Powerpoint Documents. They can directly access and save to iDisk, DropBox, and Google Docs.

- SugarSync- This service allows you to sync any files you want over multiple devices. They have a mobile app as well, but you cannot edit files in the mobile app. You still need to have a document editor on your mobile device.

CRM (Customer Relationship Management)

These are CRM's that I like. I personally use SalesForce because it is truly the best CRM that exists. It allows me to manage my clients in a very user friendly manner, and also has a task management, calendar, and mobile application. CRM's allow you to take client notes electronically, forward emails directly in to client folder, create client specific to do lists, and schedule appointments. Other than http://www.SalesForce.com, here are some other options that I like.

- Batchbook.com (http://www.batchbook.com; a social media friendly CRM)

- Heap CRM (http://heap.wbpsystems.com/)

- HighRise CRM (http://www.highrisehq.com/)

- PipelineDeals (http://www.pipelinedeals.com/)

Voicemails

There are several services that offer this, but Google has just come out with a free option.

- Google Voice - It allows you to redirect your voicemail to Google, and even create your own free Google Voicemail number. It will text message and/or email you transcriptions of voicemails, and you can create custom greetings based on who is calling. One for business. One for family. If you have 5 different phone numbers, you can set them all to use this one voicemail box. Why is this helpful? If you are somewhere where you can't talk on the phone, you can read your voicemails. You can also then email voicemails and text message voicemails to others if need be.

Task Management

Having a good task management system is absolutely imperative. With more things to do than we can every remember, we must write everything down. No question about it. There are many options out there for task management systems as well. Before embarking on changing your task management system, it would be good to read some task management and productivity theory to find which fits you best. Books like Getting Things Done, by David Allen, give great guidance here. The Getting Things Done (or GTD) system introduces a context based task management system instead of a priority based system. I will discuss in much more detail in a later chapter (see Revitalizing Your Sales Routine), but I do want to mention that in trying to eliminate stress, I personally do not agree with all of the things David Allen recommends. I take his theories and have made my own system that works for me. You can read more later. For now, here are the systems I recommend: [4]

- Remember the Milk (http://www.rememberthemilk.com/) - This is the best that exists in my opinion. More detail to follow later on this.

- Google Tasks (http://tasks.google.com/)

- OmniFocus (http://www.omnifocus.com/)

Information Gathering and Retention

- Evernote (http://www.evernote.com/) - offers a desktop, web based, and mobile service that all synchronizes that allows you to jot down notes during sales meetings and email them, capture photos to remember certain items or ads, AND utilizing the camera can take a picture of a book or article page and then does

---

[4] David Allen, Getting Things Done (Penguin Books, 2001) n. pag

text recognition, so that when you search your Evernote system, it searches the actual text in the article for what you are looking for.

Moving to 100% electronic and mobile operations is extremely helpful. You will have access to all you need always. You will have essentially a "second brain" to capture ideas instantly and make them available everywhere you are. You will never have to stop and manually sort things. The list goes on and one.

Myth #7: 100% Professionalism 100% of the Time

Truth #7: Be Yourself 100% of the Time

Okay, let me start by saying that I am NOT advocating that sales reps stop being professional. Not at all. In fact, the reason that most sales reps have jobs in the first place is because they are naturally professional. You have to be professional to succeed in business. Absolutely. However, what I have seen repeatedly are sales reps who are professional to the point that they erase their own personality during sales calls and then eventually their professionalism carries into their personal lives as well.

Now, it seems obvious, but most sales reps don't realize this. You MUST be yourself to win the respect of your clients, and to simply enjoy your job. I have spent many sales calls talking about my rock climbing and adventure experiences with clients. In fact, I have formed unbreakable business relationships/friendships because I have brought my personality and experiences into my sales. Prospects don't like to feel like "numbers", but rather like people. So let your guard down and start acting like yourself. Don't act like someone you're not.

I had a client not too long ago mention to me that he did not want me to talk to him like he was a doctor but rather as a friend. He was tired of sales reps being overly professional.

Challenge:

Here are some questions to about your prospects and/or clients:

- What are their interests?

- When is the last time I talked about non-work related things with them?

- Do I act genuinely interested in them as a person?

- Have I ever opened up to them and expressed things I am interested in or passionate about?

- Is the clothing I wear "stuffy" and "almost black-tie-formal"?

Okay. Now that you've answered those questions, I challenge you to begin probing your prospects and clients to find out if any of them share your interests. Then, begin talking about your experiences. Involve them in your life. Don't make it sound like you are just "small talking," but rather expressing genuine interest.

Not only will this change people's perspective of you, but it will help you begin to see your prospects and clients as real people, and you will begin to enjoy your job even more because you will start to see how you can be yourself ALL the time.

Myth #8: Micromanaging is Necessary to Make Sure My Team Succeeds

Truth #8: Micromanaging Your Team Reduces Your Team's Success AND Your Effectiveness

I wanted to share this myth primarily for managers. Many sales managers will read this paper and will use these points to train their sales teams. Therefore, I find it to be imperative to give some guidance on micromanaging. If you, as a manager, don't micro manage, then congratulations! Use the following advice to reinforce your stance. For those of you that do (and maybe you do and don't realize it...you should ask your reps what they think), please read the following and strongly consider changing your ways instantly.

As a manager, what I would like you to do is write down what you believe to be the top 3 responsibilities of your sales reps. Most likely, it includes FIND CUSTOMERS, SELL TO THEM, RETAIN BUSINESS. So, I can very easily make my point here. By requiring them to provide such an exorbitant amount of detail to you, you are taking away from the time that they need to be doing their actual job, which is selling.

Micromanaging actually affects the manager though, more than the reps. It causes managers to be

- Constantly stressed out

- Always feeling like they are "forgetting" something

- Juggling numerous conversations and trying to keep everyone's situations straight

- Working extra hours because they have to find time to process all the information they receive from the team

Take time to review Myths 1-7. Do you see how Micro Managing causes you to believe and practice these myths, and causes your team to believe and practice them? It makes sales a numbers game, because your team is always reporting all the number of calls etc to you. It makes you and your team multi task because there is no way that they or you have time to provide and process all the information you are requesting. It piles on the options that your team has to juggle in their minds. Your team doesn't know what to value and what not to value. It lends itself to working extra long hours. It reduces the amount of enjoyment a rep can have in their job because it limits the selling they can do. You are overworking yourself and your team.

Now OF COURSE, it is absolutely necessary to get sales reports and review strategy with your team. You are the manager after all. It is a fine line to walk indeed. You need to make sure that your team sees you as HELPFUL, and not a HINDRANCE.

Maybe your micromanaging is really a deeper issue of a lack of trust you have in others? Just a thought.

Challenge

- Write a list of all the things that you require of your reps.

- How many of those things are helping them sell?

- What things do you think you could eliminate? What things could you reduce the detail on?

- What fears do you have in doing this?

Now try to implement change. Learn to request only important information from your team and stop asking for busy work. Here's an example. Do you require detailed call logs? Why not just ask your reps to send you an email at the end of each week with the top 3 sales pitches/deals they closed that week. If they don't have anything to share, then ask why.

By following this advice, your and your team's stress will be greatly reduced. Your team's effectiveness will be increased because you will help them stop practicing Myths 1-7, and free them up to SELL!

Myth #9: I Must Take Everything Personally to Truly Be Effective

Truth #9: Business is Business. No Matter How You Look at It

In sales, it is imperative to develop relationships with prospects and clients. To me, that is one of the best things about sales. I love working with people and getting to learn things from them! However, because of this, it is so easy to lose the distinction between business and personal life.

We often allow challenges, lost business, complaints, and problems affect us personally. We carry these things around with us as if it has been an insult on us personally. We often take it out on those we love, and allow it to zap us of joy. The opposite is true as well. When we allow business to affect us personally, it changes our demeanor and clients and prospects will begin to notice that we are distracted and/or downcast. This will create a downward spiral for you.

Here is a question to ask yourself, and I know it sounds obvious: "Why do you allow business to have an impact on your personal life?"

It's a hard question to answer; and often it's one that we can't answer clearly. That should throw up a red flag. Really, the answer should be "I DON'T want to allow business issues to have an impact on my personal life."

Our job is our job. Our personal life is our life. What if you could learn to allow work to stay at work, and not bleed into your personal life? You will be much more focused in your business and sales practices. Your customers will most definitely notice it because you will always be joyful and responsive always. They will be impressed with the way you carry yourself. Your personal relationships will be greatly affected because you will no longer allow work to control your every emotion and action. Your joy in life will be greatly increased. Your sales will skyrocket.

Challenge:

1.Make the decision that for 2 weeks, you will not complain or discuss BAD things that happen at work when you are not working. So when the day ends, and you go home, NO talking about bad or disappointing things. Talk about them during the day with your significant other and/or friend, but not when you get home.

2.Of course, I am not wanting you to stop sharing bad things forever. Rather, I want you to see how much time you most likely spend complaining. By taking 2 weeks to only talk about GOOD work things, you will most likely learn to replace all the complaining, and watch your joy return.

Myth #10: Sales Success Comes From Being Constantly Recognized and Awarded

Truth #10: Having the motivation of "I want to succeed so I can live my life," will accomplish more than "I want to succeed so I can be recognized."

As a sales rep, I'm sure you have some form of President's Club, or Award Trip that you are always working toward achieving. It is the mark of ultimate sales success, right? Well, it's partly right. One of the things that is so important to recognize is that as sales reps, we can so easily find our self-worth and fulfillment in whether we are awarded or celebrated for our success. I believe that it's time for sales reps to stop finding their fulfillment in these things, and instead find their self-worth and fulfillment in whether they are living the life they desire to live.

Challenge:

Take some time to think of the governing values/vision of your life.

- What do you see yourself as in 5 years? 10 years?

- What is most important to you in your life?

- What values and beliefs govern (or should be governing) your every action and goal?

Now, look at your life and see if the current path you are on is in line with the values and visions you mention. Are your current work practices helping you accomplish what is most important in your life? Are you on track to accomplish what you want to see yourself as in 5-10 years? Are you in line with your values?

Remember, that we work to live. We are not (or shouldn't be) living to work. At the end of the day, if you align your work practices up with your ultimate life goal, visions, and purposes, you will find more contentment, happiness, and satisfaction than you ever will find in receiving recognition from others. By changing your practices, you will begin to close more sales as well because you will enjoy your life more and be much more focused. *Having the motivation of "I want to succeed so I can live my life," will accomplish MUCH more than "I want to succeed so I can be recognized."*

Now, I'm not saying that you should not be striving towards great achievement. Or that you shouldn't work to be the best. On the contrary. I believe that if you follow my advice on changing your thinking about Myths 1-9, you will be taking steps to achieving greater things, living your life, and closing more sales.

Chapter 5: Revitalizing Your Sales Routine

Congratulations! You made it through the meat of the book and the most mentally challenging part. Many people, when I have discussed and/or presented the Sales Myths and their corresponding belief corrections, have expressed to me that it left them feeling stressed out and unsure which one to start with first! That is understandable. So now that you have read all the sales myths, I want to help you learn how to apply it to your life and how to structure your days and weeks so that you can be alive, effective, and fully of joy at the same time!

Remember what I said in the beginning chapters: You must first start with the heart. So starting with the belief changes is most important. If you do not first change your beliefs, the practical advice and guidelines I provide will prove to be ineffective.

At the end of this chapter, you will be able to:

•Define your plan of action for applying one myth at at time

•Know how to structure your calendar in the most effective way that guarantees your time will be used most wisely and most effectively

•Maintain a system that will make sure you never forget opportunities that you are working on with your clients and/or leads

•Know how to prevent interruptions in your day, so that you can accomplish the work you need to

It is necessary that I point out that as you read the following chapter, you will probably say to yourself, "Why am I being given SO much to do? I thought this book was about eliminating stress, not creating more!" Allow me to answer that by saying I never said it wouldn't take work to change in all of these ways and implement a new system. If you are committed to eliminating stress, enjoying life more, and ultimately closing more sales, you will need to work HARD at developing practices and principles that will lead you to that point. Knowing that the result will be a stress free and happier life should motivate you to work hard in the meantime towards that end. In the next chapter, I will give you some practical guidelines on how to add PERSONAL Life back in to your life. Let's get started with the practical sales changes to make.

I personally take time to revisit these myths myself, and review my practices because it is so easy to get sidetracked and lose focus on what is truly important. So this is not a once and done thing. It is something we all must work on frequently to make sure we are living life and performing our jobs as an Alive Sales Rep.

STEP 1: Tackle One Myth at a Time

Here are the 10 Sales Truths again. Take time to read through them slowly.

1. Sales is an Ideal Customer Game

2. Uni-Tasking Will Get More Done

3. More Options Will Lead to More Confusion

4. Cold Calling is Dead

5. Work is Most Effective if It Is Done During Work Hours

6. Paper Based Organization Systems Will Leave You More Confused and Less Effective

7. Be Yourself 100% of the Time

8. Micromanaging Your Team Reduces Their Success and Your Effectiveness

9. Business is Business...No Matter How You Look at It

10. Having the motivation of "I want to succeed so I can live my life," will accomplish more than "I want to succeed so I can be recognized."

Now look back at them again and rank them in order of importance to you. The first one on your list should be the one that you know you need to focus on changing ASAP. The last one on the list should be one that maybe you already believe and apply, or are close to adopting.

You now have your #1 Belief to Focus on Changing. What you need to do is take 1 month to try to focus your efforts on changing that belief. At the same time, take 1 month to focus on making your STRONGEST belief on the list (#10) even STRONGER. The idea is to work on your weaknesses and at the same time make your strengths stronger. Put these items on your calendar as reminders, so you always remember to reflect on them. If it takes you less than a month to change, GREAT....then move on to the next one. If you get to a month and you notice decent change, still move on to the next belief. You can continue to go back and reevaluate. You need to make sure that you are not too fixated on one myth and thereby neglect the others.

Everyone's plan of action for how you work on changing those beliefs will look different. Remember, in each of the myths in the previous chapter, I have given some starting advice on how to begin to apply those beliefs to your mind and life. Start there and then continue to develop your own plan as you see fit. It will take discipline to change your beliefs, so be patient.

Keep in mind, that as you work on changing beliefs that have become so prevalent in the business and sales world today, there will be people who doubt your actions, or think that you are ridiculous. Just remember, that you know what the end outcome will be and you simply need to persevere. You know that in the end you will be MORE successful. So keep pushing ahead in to the paradigm change.

It'll probably be helpful if I give you some examples so that you can see what it looks like to practice these things. I will share with you what my biggest belief change was that got me on the path to developing this paradigm and ultimately writing this book.

Multitasking. I have always been a multitasker. In fact, a friend of mine once gave me Dave Crenshaw's book preaching against multitasking, Multitasking, and I immediately handed it back and said, "That's ridiculous...the whole reason we have so much technology and information at our fingertips is so we CAN multitask." I quickly dismissed it until a year or so later I was sitting at my computer and had so many things to do that I had no idea where to start. I seriously felt like my head was going to explode. It was at that moment that I thought, "I just have to pick one project and work on it, and nothing else until it is done." It was truly at that moment that I realized my problem was not focusing on one thing at a time, but rather trying to jump between tasks. For example, I may have a long email to write, but while I am writing the email, I have to look up something on a website to include in the email. While the page is loading, I might try to sort through other emails, and then the chain continues. When I realized that I did this, I immediately tried to keep my focus on one thing at a time and not multitask. It was then that I remembered Crenshaw's book and I read it in one sitting. Definitely read that book if you are a chronic multitasker!

So figure out what your weakness is and tackle it. Look online to see if anyone has written books (like Crenshaw did for Multitasking) on the thing you struggle with.

NOW...most importantly, focus on your #1 STRENGTH. Mine is #6...having an electronic organization system. I love finding ways technology can help me, so I continued to research new ways to add these things to my business and life. I could make revisions to this book daily with all the new things I find out there. So...don't forget to continue to develop your strengths.

STEP 2: Organize Your Prospects, Clients, and Territory into a Meaningful System

This will most likely take some significant time to do. Of course, you could do a haphazard job and quickly throw information together. That will only leave you more confused. So I encourage you to schedule a few appointments on your calendar where you will do nothing except work on building a system that will be meaningful to you in helping you keep track of your clients, prospects, and territory.

I'm going to assume that if you've come this far in reading this book, that you are willing to make serious changes in your practices. So if you don't already use a CRM, I encourage you to subscribe to one of the services online. Again, I recommend Batchbook (http://www.batchbook.com), since it is great for personal use. Many companies have CRMs that are more robust like SalesForce, or Sage. If you already use a CRM, that's great! I hope that my recommendations below will serve you well fine tuning your system. Now, let me just add, that if you have thousands of leads, chances are you first need to look back to Myth 1 and get rid of those that do not fit your target market, so that you make the next steps easier and more beneficial for yourself.

1. Make sure you have all relevant demographic information for each contact and lead. This will take a lot of time, but it is so important that you have address, phone, fax, email, website, blog address, etc for each lead. You will be much more effective this way. Also, be sure to have your decision maker listed for each company you may be selling to. If you find that you don't have some of this information on hand, that gives you some items to research and follow up on. It is important to have a good grasp on everyone in your system.

2. Make sure you have valuable descriptions of each lead. This also will take a significant amount of time. You will want to have notes entered for each lead that describes why they are a lead. Maybe you feel like you have all this information in your mind already. That's not good enough. Not only will this help

you have info on each client, but it will give you a chance to think through each lead in your system, and will help you once you get a bigger book of leads to be able to quickly reference why each lead is there in the first place. I know that I have benefited greatly from this. I have been preparing to make a sales presentation, and was reviewing notes on previous calls I made on this lead. I noticed in my original "Lead Description" that I had made notes regarding some interests the practice manager had that I forgot about. I added it to my presentation and it helped me close the sale!

3. Have a good note taking system. It is important that you don't write a note for EVERY action you have with a lead. You don't need to write "cold call unsuccessful," or "left voicemail, " etc.; you should be writing important information such as "Cold call unsuccessful because they...", so that you can reference these notes in the future. Notes should not be used to remind you that "Oh, I left a voicemail on that day," , etc. You will develop a separate system for that. More to follow.

4. Develop a tagging system. Having a good method for tagging leads and prospects is essential. I have tags called Hot, Warm, and Cold, to mark which leads I need to go after. Hot means that they are close to moving towards a 90 day close window. Warm means that I need to focus on them, and Cold means that I've called on them, but no real progress in sight. I have additional tags such as Service Issue, Pricing Issue, Recommendation, Compliment, Request, and New Information as well. I use these

tags to mark various notes and/or emails and phone calls from clients that need to be kept track of. For example, if I get an email complaining about a price issue, I would tag it with Pricing Issue, so that I can easily keep track of all pricing issues. I have tags for each product or service I offer as well. I run several companies, so I use a tag for each company name so that I know what contact belongs to what company as well. The important thing about having a tag system is that it allows you to get instant access to valuable information when you need it. If you want to see what leads are hot and are interested in abcd product, you can filter by those tags and get that information.

5. Determine what criteria moves a lead from Lead Status to Deal Status. Most CRMs will have their own terminology regarding status of leads, but many use the title of Deal for a lead that has a high probability of closing. In other words, those leads that become deals are leads that you feel comfortable putting in to your sales pipeline. It is necessary for you to have criteria that will make you move a lead from "Leads" to "Deals." For example, does a lead become a deal just because they returned your phone call? Does a lead become a deal because you had a meeting with them? Well, if a phone call and/or meeting means that they will most likely close, then yes. You need to determine what makes a lead a good candidate for closing. A criteria I use is those leads that I would list if someone said to me, "Tell me the accounts that you will you close within the next 30, 60, and 90 days,"

6. Develop a CRM Review Process. You can build a great CRM system, but if you don't have a meaningful way to use it, then it is just a pile of information. It is important to have a scheduled, step by step review process 1 to 2 times per week so that you can be certain you are not missing out on opportunities. I have developed a list of questions that I ask myself every Monday morning and every Friday afternoon to help me dig through information gathered and therefore plan appropriately. Here are those questions:

•What information did I add to my prospects notes this week?

•Can any of these prospects be turned in to hot leads

•Out of my hot leads, what steps do I need to take next on each of them this week to move them to deal and/or close?

•Out of my deals, do their close dates need to be changed?

•What steps do I need to take next with my deals to bring them to close?

•Do I have any new prospects that are not yet in my CRM system?

•Do I have scheduled visits and/or cold calls built in to my week for each hot prospect and deal?

•What prospects and/or deals require a phone call or email today?

This process may seem pointless to you, but I can assure you that it helps you clearly think through each target and makes sure you are not dropping the ball or missing out on any opportunities.

STEP 3: Develop a Task Management System that Literally Brings You Peace of Mind

Now this section could have an entire book written about it. WAIT! Actually, a full book has been written about this topic: David Allen's book <u>Getting Things Done</u> (GTD). As I mentioned earlier, this is a great book, and is great for someone who wants a very detailed system for task management.

I want to take a moment to tell you my story of using the GTD system. I used GTD for many years because I thought it was the only and best system that existed. I spent countless time every day organizing tasks, making sure I had all my tasks recorded correctly, and reviewing my systems. I realized at one point that instead of causing me less stress and anxiety, the GTD system was creating more work for me and more stress. So I developed my own system that is a hybrid between GTD and my own personal needs. If you have never used a task management system, or just have a haphazard system, I'd recommend reading Getting Things Done and seeing if it works for you. If nothing else, it will help you see what you are missing in task management. Then over time, you can adapt to your needs.

The whole idea is that by having an effective task management and life management system, it is basically providing you with a second brain to keep track of all these to-dos and wish-lists, so that you don't have to and can have peace of mind. Please take my recommendation to do this.

There are some key points that I want to point out about the importance of developing such a system. First I want to share some of the points that David Allen makes in his book Getting Things Done, and then I will take these points, mix them with me "real life sales experience of task management," and give some consolidated points of advice.

Tips Gleaned from GTD:

1. Sales Reps Have Too Much to Think About. Every cold call you make and every meeting you have provides you with an innumerable amount of tasks to keep track of. On top of that, you have requests from managers and other sales reps such as reports to email, phone calls to make, emails to send, etc. Then you also have things YOU are waiting on OTHER people for. How in the world can you keep track of all of this without constantly feeling like you are forgetting something? It is very hard to do so. This is one of the greatest causes of stress because it is hard to think about the next steps (i.e. strategize) because you are petrified to add more tasks to your list because you already feel overwhelmed, and feel that you are always forgetting something or missing a detail.

2. Sales Reps Need a Second Brain. Having a task management system such as <u>Getting Things Done</u> (GTD), will allow you to keep track of Emails To Send, Phone Calls to Make, Waiting On Items, Someday/Maybe Wishlists, and more. It is not a software system, it is a methodology. You can apply the methodology to most software systems. One of the things that David Allen discusses is the importance of having an Inbox. I personally use Remember the Milk on my iPhone and computer to keep track of my tasks. Whenever I have a new project arise or have a new idea, I record it in my inbox to be reviewed later. The beauty of this is that you can be confident that you wrote it down, and when you sit down to review your inbox, you will remember it and plan for it then, but for now, you can be done thinking about it. Then when it comes time to process your inbox, one of David Allen's Key Principles is that you plan out a project in full, in successive tasks. So instead of writing "Set up new client" on your list, your list may look something like this:

- Fill Out New Forms (To-do on computer list)

- Send in forms to Mr. Smith (Emails to Send List)

- Approved by Mr. Smith (Waiting On List)

- Order Supplies (Phone Calls to Make List)

You can have due dates assigned to each task, and you will then make sure you are tracking each part of a project. The whole idea is that if you keep track of every task, you never have to think about it.

There are myriad of other ideas and principles David Allen shares. Please buy the book. [5]

Brandon's GTD and Alive Sales Rep Task Management Hybrid Points (some day maybe I'll pick a shorter name for it!)

1. Build a context based task management system. Whatever choice you make for systems, make sure it at least gives you the ability to have tasks be context based. That way you can tag a task as "phone", "email", "home", or "work", and can quickly pull up all tasks that are phone calls, emails, etc. This will make you much more efficient. My favorite thing about this is that I can tag tasks with a person's name, and then when I am talking with that person, I can pull up their name and see everything that I want to discuss with them.

2. Record tasks that will help you understand what the next steps are. For me, I just need one reminder for a project, but for others maybe you need multiple steps written down. For example, if I write up a task that says "Set up new IT services for client ABC," I will know what to do, so I don't have to write multiple tasks. But if you would need to type out who to email etc, then that is fine as well. This is where I feel like GTD is burdensome...it recommends writing down everything.

---

[5] David Allen, Getting Things Done (Penguin Books, 2001) n. pag

3. It is very important to maintain the Inbox concept that GTD discusses. When you have a new idea or thought, write it down in your Inbox to be processed later so that you will not forget it.

There is obviously much more to say on task management. Take time to read GTD, and go from there.

STEP 4: Construct a Calendar that Will Enable You to Better Use Your Time

We all use calendars. If you are still using a paper calendar, chances are THAT is the reason you are stressed out the most! It is hard to use a calendar for maximum efficiency if it is all handwritten. So make that change NOW. Start using an electronic calendar, whether it is on your company's exhange (Outlook) server, Outlook itself, Apple's iCal, Gmail, etc.

We are all familiar with using a calendar to make appointments with clients, or to schedule conference calls. You may be unfamiliar with using a calendar to schedule PERSONAL work time. I use my calendar for the following things, along with appointment scheduling , etc.:

    •CRM Reviews

    •Weekly Task Reviews

    •Phone Call Returning

•Email Sending

•Marketing Organizing

•Sales Call Planning

•Personal Fitness Time

•Personal Reading Time

These are all items that we tend to think "When will I ever have time to...", and get stressed out about it. By using your calendar to schedule these important items, you will ALWAYS have time to do it. So for example, I schedule time for myself at 10:00am, 1:00pm, and 4:00pm for 15 minutes each day to return phone calls. If someone calls or talks to me and says "Hey can you meet me at 1:00pm?", I say "How about 1:15?" Same for CRM planning , etc. Items on my calendar for my own productivity are JUST as important and concrete as appointments with clients , etc. I truly believe that if it wasn't for these scheduled times, I would not have as many appointments with clients!

So go ahead and start scheduling yourself out. You can set up recurring meetings/appointments, and begin to see a tremendous difference.

STEP 5: Get Rid of All the Extra Stuff You Carry Around With You That You Will Never Need

Have you ever looked around at all your "Sales Stuff" and felt overwhelmed? Chances are, 80% of the things you have loaded in your car and/or in your office you will NEVER use and therefore is just causing CLUTTER.

Most of the time, the reason we keep so many marketing flyers, files etc laying around is because we think we may need them. If you remember above I discussed using a CRM. That will ELIMINATE your need for paper files on clients. As for other things, I would encourage you to go through your files and get rid of EVERYTHING you haven't used in a month. I can almost bet you money that you will not use them. If you do need it again, you can always go back to get whatever you cleaned out.

In my sales job, I have literally 150 different marketing flyers I could be carrying around with me. It is easy to feel like I need to have several of each of those available at any given moment to give to clients. So I could get a TON of crates and fill my car with thousands of sheets of paper. There is NO way I will do that, and NO way that I need to. Instead, I took time to look at each marketing flyer and think about when I would need it. I narrowed down my flyers to a stack of 20 "Must Haves." I then took one of each, put it in a binder, and kept it in my car. When I talked with a client, if they wanted to review information on something we were discussing, I showed them the flyer in my binder. If they wanted it as a leave behind, I would leave it for them, and simply write down on my task system, under "Things to Do at the Office," that I needed to restock my binder with that flyer.

Think about how FREE you would feel if you threw away all that extra clutter. Not to mention how much time it would save you when you take your family somewhere in your car and you no longer have to spend 30 minutes cleaning out all the work supplies from your car!

STEP 6: Find Someone to Confide In That Will Keep You Accountable

It is an ancient truth that people are happier and more successful when they involve others in their lives and ideas. I encourage you to share these new plans you have for your work life with someone else, and ask them to keep you accountable. Maybe have a weekly conversation with that person where you know they will ask you how you are doing with making progress in each of these new areas. They can ask you what new successes you have, and what struggles you have. By sharing with someone, it can often help you think of new ways to change and develop. Also, you will have a great sense of satisfaction in developing a new, strong relationship.

As a caveat to this, it is also important that you make sure you do not surround yourself with people who have a negative impact on you. This would include discouraging people, pessimists, and people who generally are "naysayers." There is a big difference between someone who helps you question whether or not an action is a good one and someone who is always a naysayer saying, "You could never do xyz." Be careful who you surround yourself with. It can truly make or break you.

Chapter 6: Bring Your Personal Life Back to Life

I hope that you have been challenged in many ways by reading this book. I wanted to finish the book with a chapter on how to revitalize your personal life, as you begin to eliminate stress in your work life and begin to free up some time. In fact, it is this very thing, the revitalization of your personal life and the awakening of a new enjoyment of life, that will motivate you to make all the business and sales changes mentioned above.

So, here are some simple things you can do to begin to revitalize your personal life. It easily gets addicting, and can be tempting to keep heaping things on your plate to add to your "Personal Enjoyment List", but don't be too hasty; you can get overwhelmed by all of the things you want to add back in to your personal life. I think that following these steps will be a great start.

What are the top 3 things you wish to revitalize?

I can pretty much guarantee that you can think of the top 3 things you would enjoy doing again or doing more of in your personal life. Maybe it's simply reading more books, exercising more, or something basic. Or maybe it's learn a new language, or take pilot lessons. Whatever it is, write the top 3 things down that you want to see come back in to your personal life. This list is VERY important. It is what is going to drive you to be become an Alive Sales Rep. Write it down in several places, so you can always be reminded of them.

What are the barriers to starting to pursue these things?

Now, look back at those 3 things and figure out what the barriers to starting to pursue these things are. Why haven't you been able to read like you wanted to? Why haven't you been able to exercise? What is getting in the way of [fill in the blank]? So, did you discover that work or work related stresses are to blame? I bet that it was present somewhere in your reasons. Let's say that you want to exercise more, and after careful thought, you realize that the barrier to pursuing this is that you start working at 6am every day, and can't find the time to exercise. Your barrier is that you are overworking. Sound familiar? IT SHOULD! It's one of the myths listed above. Do you see how changing your perspective and beliefs in regard to work can drastically impact all of your life?

Come Up With a Plan to Remove the Barriers

Now you need to come up with a plan to remove the barriers. When it comes down to it, it probably won't be that hard. In my own life, I set out to become proficient at jazz guitar. I simply changed my morning routine, and now practice jazz guitar 15 minutes every morning. It has made a GREAT impact. So don't feel like your changes need to be drastic! Simply come up with a barrier removing plan for each of the barriers you listed for your personal life list.

Same determination and drive you have with work

Now, you need to do the most important part. START LIVING YOUR LIFE. You need to pursue your personal life and passions with just as much drive and fervor as you do your work. Can you feel the difference that will make? I'm sure you will quickly begin to realize that you have been missing out on truly enjoying life for far too long.

Care for Your Body First and Foremost

In Appendix 1, I took time to write in detail about the dangers of stress and how it can truly harm us physically through increases in Cortisol levels. Take time to read Appendix 1. Here, I just want to discuss the importance of caring for your body overall. Remember, we are not created as half spiritual beings and half physical beings. Our physical and spiritual selves are intertwined and therefore we need to make sure we care equally for them. As you read this book, I'm sure you learned many ways that you need to change your thinking, and reduce stress mentally. Keep in mind that if you don't also care for your physical self, you will not have the harmony you are looking for.

Developing some form of an exercise plan is essential. A simple plan is to add in aerobic exercise 3 times per week, and some form of resistance training (weights, etc.) 2 times per week. Then add a 30-60 minute session of Yoga once per week. You can sign up on YogaToday.com, and get Yoga Classes emailed to you so you can do them in the comfort of your own home!

Why is all of this beneficial? Here is a quick synopsis:

1. Aerobic exercise gives you endorphins, and builds your metabolism, ultimately making you have less "ups and downs," as well as making you feel better about yourself. Running in the morning is a great substitute for that extra cup of coffee.

2. Weight training increases your human growth hormone level, which affects your cortisol production, sugar absorption, and for men, your testosterone levels. It will help stress go down.

3. Yoga helps your body release tension. High cortisol levels from stress can create muscular tension and pain. Release it through Yoga. When you do your first session, upon conclusion I bet you will feel this abnormal energy rush/peaceful sensation in your body. It is because toxins are being released. Yoga is important to a training program.

Of course, eating well, sleeping well, not drinking excess alcohol, and not consuming too much caffeine are all an important part of caring for your body.

Learn What Make You Happy and Makes You Satisfied and Pursue It

Have you ever taken the time to think about what truly makes you happy, or what situation/occurrence would make you feel satisfied?

If you are bogged down by work, chances are you don't take much time to look at the horizon.

So...give yourself 20 minutes to sit down and think about times in your life when you were truly happy. Write them down. Then write down under each of those things 5 ways you felt in those circumstances. Make it all a combination of work and personal life. Now go back and look at the lists and see if you feel that way about your life and situation right now. If you don't, what can you do to bring back those feelings? Change jobs? Shift your work load? Take on new projects? Delegate more work? The possibilities are endless. But take some time to make sure you are truly happy and if you are not, do something to change it right away.

Our lives are not about work. We are first and foremost individuals given a marvelous gift of life. Make sure that we are enjoying it. I personally am at a point now where I enjoy my life greatly, and work is a very enjoyable part of it to me because I have found a perfect balance.

Conclusion

One of the greatest fears I have in writing this book is that someone will interpret it wrong and think that I am advocating a lazy approach to work. I hope that in all I have said, I have made it clear that that is not the case at all. The opposite is true in fact. I want people to work hard and smart, but to make sure that they are not sacrificing their personal lives at the same time.

I love selling and business and teaching others. I have truly discovered that by changing my beliefs about work and sales, that my success skyrockets. When I was falsely believing all the myths that I listed above, I was far less successful. But now I have watched my entire life change for the good. All I want is to share that excitement and joy with others.

In the past, I didn't see work as enjoyable. I had a desire to enjoy my life and saw work as a stressful obstacle. After much trial and error, I learned all of the things I have described in this book, and now see work as an enjoyable part of life.

So remember, this book is about becoming a more successful sales rep by changing your beliefs and practices.

So I hope you begin your paradigm shifting, life changing journey TODAY, towards becoming an Alive Sales Rep. Your life is about to get incredibly better.

Appendix 1: The Dangers of Stress

I know that I don't need to spend too much time telling you that stress is bad, or that you should get rid of it. You probably already hate being stressed out simply because it makes you restless and gives you that "my head is going to explode" feeling. However, I wanted to briefly mentioned some things you might not know about stress, just to really get you thinking about the need we have to get rid of it.

Several years ago, I went to the doctor because I noticed that my heart would get these odd, strong, irregular beats during the day. After a few tests, it was determined that it was stress related. I began a journey at that point to reduce stress, and started learning about the true physical dangers of it. One of the most intriguing things to me was that the negative impacts of stress actually make a sales rep worse at their job! The big ones that I want to point out, that I'm sure will strike a tone with every rep out there are that stress will make you forget things, make you less energetic, and will make you fat. You don't want any of those things right?

I want to talk about some of these side effects in detail before diving in to the rest of the book because I want you to feel a true desire and burden to eliminate stress in your life.

This is what I learned:

What is one big characteristic that sales reps share? STRESS! And what happens when your body is stressed out? Your adrenal gland releases cortisol. I wanted to take some time to show you what exactly cortisol does.

Cortisol serves many purposes, but I wanted to highlight a few here. Cortisol does the following:

1. Helps your body metabolize glucose
2. Helps insulin release to control and maintain blood sugar
3. Releases into your body when you are stressed and provides an adrenaline rush, or fight or flight response.

I can think of plenty of instances, such as hanging by my finger tips while rock climbing, facing a possibly life threatening fall, when my adrenaline gave me extra strength and really helped me. It is not always helpful when you are not truly facing a life threatening situation, but your body doesn't know that. Having that adrenaline rush to carry you through difficult parts of your day is important, but how often do you feel stressed out ALL day and ALL night? Fairly often I'm sure. The problem with that is your body never returns to it's rest state/normal cortisol level state, because constant stress will constantly release cortisol, and that begins to have serious negative effects on you.

What does high cortisol cause?

High Cortisol causes:

1. Decrease mental function and capacity
2. Decreased insulin sensitivity
3. Decreased metabolism of glucose
4. Increase in abdominal fat.

Now read that list again. It is scary to think that stress decreases mental function, which will make you feel more stressed out because your mind can't handle the stress, and it creates a vicious cycle. Not only that, but you will begin to forget things, and you won't be able to perform as well in your job. Think about a time you have had a stressful morning, then sit down in a meeting with a potential client. Did you feel like you didn't know what questions to ask, or how to respond to objections? Did you leave the meeting feeling like you usually are better and just couldn't figure out why you were underperforming? Well...the answer is stress and cortisol. Can you start to see how dangerous constant stress is?

Also, you will have less energy because your body cannot process glucose (sugar) as quickly. And what happens then? Increase in abdominal fat.

Why the increase in abdominal fat? Abdominal fat comes from eating sugars and carbohydrates that are high on the glycemic index, or just from having a diet high in carbohydrates. Your body converts these sugars in to fat and primarily stores them in the abdominal area. Therefore, if you are stressed out, and have high cortisol, your body is hindered in its ability to control blood sugar with insulin, and hindered in its ability to metabolize sugar, and therefore much more readily converts sugar in to fat. Sugars that you may have once had no problem converting to muscle glycogen, you are now converting in to fat because your metabolism has dropped.

And what does that cause? Well abdominal fat is a leading cause of heart disease because abdominal fat is where LP(a) Cholesterol is produced (small particles...the most dangerous ones).

Also, abdominal fat then makes you gain weight, which makes it harder to exercise. Less muscle glycogen due to decreased insulin sensitivity and glucose metabolism, makes it harder to exercise. So you stop exercising. Weight gain ensues.

What happens when you are stressed? You probably eat and drink more, and usually eat and drink a lot of carbohydrates, which, as you read above, will not be converted properly and you will gain weight.

Here's an amazing thing...reducing sugar intake actually helps reduce your cortisol levels and can help you reduce the stress you experience.

SO...how can you get your body back in control? Here are some recommendations:

1. Start de-stressing yourself and your work schedule. This is the main reason I wrote The Alive Sales Rep, and you will find many ways in the next few chapters to begin reducing stress.

2. Eat a diet of low glycemic load (Glycemic Load=Glycemic Index x #Carbs in a Serving, so if bread has a Glycemic Index of 70, and there are 25g carbs in one slice, the

glycemic load would be .70x25, or 17.5) for 30 days. Maintaining low blood sugar will help your body reduce it's secretion of cortisol. This means eating foods low on the glycemic index: no bread, no sugars, no fruit, no grains, no chips. You can get MORE than enough carbohydrates from eating a lot of legumes. So make an egg white omelet for breakfast with spinach and a ton of black beans. For lunch, make black bean or lentil soup. Make a burrito bowl, with chicken, black beans, onions, peppers, avocados (allowable!), salsa, and lettuce for dinner. Eat raw nuts, have a soy protein shake. Most importantly….STOP CONSUMING DAIRY. By changing your diet in this way, you will be helping your body change it's metabolism and increase its sugar maintenance just by your eating habits.

3. Start exercising! I would recommend a combination of aerobic exercise, and eventually getting in to CrossFit. (www.Crossfit.com). For aerobic exercise, try to run intervals, where you sprint hard for 30 seconds, then jog for 1.5 minutes. Do this for 30 minutes 3 or 4 times per week and you will drive your metabolism higher. As for CrossFit, the more you develop your muscles, the more your body will learn to process Glucose and store muscle glycogen.

4. Sleep more! Plain and simple. Consider taking a melatonin pill before bed

5. Start practicing Yoga for peace, relaxation, and fitness. For a good way to get started, check out www.yogatoday.com

6. Do not drink caffeine after noon, and do not use 5 Hour Energy. Caffeine, but ESPECIALLY 5 HOUR ENERGY, creates a false fight or flight response, and triggers Cortisol. Too much 5 Hour Energy can actually deplete your adrenal system. Stay away from it. It is NOT good for you.

7. All of these things will help restore your body back to normal cortisol levels, reduce stress significantly, improve mental capacity, and help you get on the path to weight loss and better overall health.

Appendix 2: 49 Sales Tips

I created a series on my blog called 49 Sales Tips which gives several quick points and tips on sales, some of which can be found throughout The Alive Sales Rep, and some of which are unique to this list.. So here is a list of those 49 Tips. On my blog, 2 paragraphs of additional detail are written for each of these. So check out www.TheAliveSalesRep.com for more detail on these sales tips.

So why 49 Tips, and why is it broken up by weekday? Well, it is believed that people can remember no more than 7 things at once, and I thought having 7 tips per day for 7 days would be the perfect formula! Enjoy.

Monday

1. Exercise

2. Take a lunch break

3. Perform a regular 80/20 analysis

4. Leave out the kitchen sink

5. Don't believe in the "Numbers Game" lie

6. Know, in explicit detail, who your ideal prospect and customer is

7. Stay away from multitasking

Tuesday

8. Use online tools, such as RescueTime.com, to force yourself to stop multitasking

9. Stop cold calling and start value-calling

10. Apply Parkinson's Law

11. Don't find fulfillment in recognition

12. Don't be afraid of change

13. When working on personal change, take it one step at a time

14. Don't be let down or discouraged by rejection, but allow it to motivate you to try harder on your next call

Wednesday

15. Don't let a competitor's win depress or discourage you. Use it as an opportunity to learn how you could've better positioned your product or service.

16. Use social media tools to market yourself and the value you bring in your territory. Don't use it to market the company you work for...the company you work for should be marketing themselves.

17. Don't work for a company or sell a product that you believe is inferior to your competitors or competitors' product/service.

18. Always sell with integrity.

19. Learn to ask questions.

20. Use electronic organization methods and stay away from paper.

21. Make reading an essential part of your day.

Thursday

22. Be persistent. You never know when you will walk in to the right place at the right time.

23. Express your career desires to the people you work for.

24. If you work for yourself (or your own company), make sure your passion for what you do rubs off on your sales reps and employees.

25. If you are a sales manager, don't micromanage

26. Don't energize yourself with caffeine throughout the day. Stop drinking caffeine at 10am and you will watch your stress level rapidly decline.

27. Don't check your email before bed. Your will subconsciously think about it throughout the night and you will not be 100% the next day due to lack of sleep.

28. In the myriad of options and products/services you sell, find what you are most passionate about and focus on it. The customers will see and feel the difference and buy from you.

Friday

29. The old saying is true..."The customer is always right." Make sure you never argue with a customer to prove that you are right, when you know you are.

30. Be confident when making calls. Instead of saying, "I was wondering if I could speak with Mr. Smith," say something like, "I need to..." or "I would like to." It will come across much better.

31. Develop task management systems that work for you...don't just adopt someone else's system.

32. Batch important tasks. For example, schedule "Computer Time" throughout the day so that you aren't constantly working on your computer.

33. Don't be afraid to go for the biggest clients. They chose the competitor because the competitor wasn't afraid. You shouldn't be afraid either.

34. Don't take things to seriously. Try to have a light-hearted attitude. It will come across to your clients, and will also reduce stress.

35. Never think that anything is impossible.

Saturday

36. Your health is your most precious possession. Take good care of yourself by exercise and eating well. It will make you feel better and will reduce stress significantly.

37. Never neglect your personal life. Make sure your work is not erasing the things you once enjoyed from your life.

38. Put a high priority on building relationships with clients, the people you work with, and the people in your non work life.

39. Be accountable to someone for all of your actions.

40. Remember what you were like mentally and emotionally at your best moments, and try to never let those feelings and emotions go. It will help you always perform at your best.

41. Realize that you will not always have outstanding months. Learn to be ok with not being on top all the time.

42. You have a purpose for being here on this earth. Try to not be myopically focused on work, but look at all of life so that you can truly enjoy life.

Sunday

43. If you find that there are administrative tasks that bog you down, make every effort to figure out new ways to reduce or eliminate these draining tasks.

44. Are you able to use a virtual assistant for any of your cumbersome work related tasks?

45. Set personal goals for yourself so that you are motivated to sell hard and sell a lot. By having goals you are working towards, you will be driven to succeed.

46. Can you think of 3 things you have done recently that "broke the mold?" If not, you need to stop acting like all other sales reps and start being unique.

47. Schedule your day, every day. Don't just make sales calls "flying by the seat of your pants." Fail to plan, plan to fail.

48. Read the book "Transcend" on extending life.

49. Work to Live, Don't Live to Work

Workbooks

The following section contains small worksheets to help you, the reader, apply each of the 10 Sales Myths. Re-read the "Challenges" listed under each myth and your memory will be refreshed as to what these worksheets are asking you to do

Worksheet 1: Make it an Ideal Customer Game

What characteristics does your ideal customer have?

What prospects that you are currently working on do not fit your ideal customer profile?

Worksheet 2: Do Not Multitask

Go back to myth 2 and review the instructions for the Multitasking is a Lie exercise. The space below is for you to give it a try.

Multitasking Attempt:

— — — — — — — — — — — — — — — — —

— — — — — — — — — — — — — — — — —

Unitasking Attempt

— — — — — — — — — — — — — — — — —

— — — — — — — — — — — — — — — — —

Worksheet 3: Get Rid of All the Clutter From Your Sales Presentations

What items are you carrying in to sales meetings and/or presentations with you? List them ALL below:

Which of those items have you not used in:

A Week:

A Month:

Ever:

Worksheet 4: Cold Calling Is Dead

What kind of articles or materials can you begin to provide your prospects with so that you become truly valuable to them:

Worksheet 5: Working Regular Hours

2 Week Time Tracking

Time Spent Working:

•M-

•T-

•W-

•Th-

•F-

•Weekend-

Things Left Undone:

New Enforced Work Hours Only Schedule:

Hours worked outside of work hours:

Things Left Undone:

Worksheet 6: Eliminate Paper

What tasks or responsibilities do you still use paper based systems for?

Write down technology that appeals to you that could replace your paper based systems listed above:

Worksheet 7: Be Yourself

Write down the top 5 character qualities you think are great about yourself personally (not business oriented):

Write down the last time in a work environment/ presentation you displayed each of those characteristics above:

Worksheet 8: Stop Micromanaging

Write a list of all the things that you require of your reps.

How many of those things are helping them sell?

What things do you think you could eliminate? What things could you reduce the detail on?

What fears do you have in doing this?

Worksheet 9: Don't Take Everything Personally

What are the things you get most upset about in your job?

How many of those things affect your personal life (joy, rest, etc.) outside of normal work hours?

Why do you think you are taking these things personally?

Worksheet 10: Be Motivated by a Fulfilling Life

What do you see yourself as in 5 years? 10 years?

What is most important to you in your life?

What values and beliefs govern (or should be governing) your every action and goal?